YOUR KNOWLEDGE HAS VALUE

Luis Enrique Ponce Goyochea

Towards a Greater Depression?

GRIN Verlag

Bibliografische Information der Deutschen Nationalbibliothek:

Die Deutsche Bibliothek verzeichnet diese Publikation in der Deutschen National-
bibliografie; detaillierte bibliografische Daten sind im Internet über http://dnb.d-
nb.de/ abrufbar.

Imprint:

Copyright © 2013 GRIN Verlag GmbH
Druck und Bindung: Books on Demand GmbH, Norderstedt Germany
ISBN: 978-3-656-51794-8

This book at GRIN:

http://www.grin.com/en/e-book/233074/towards-a-greater-depression

GRIN - Your knowledge has value

Der GRIN Verlag publiziert seit 1998 wissenschaftliche Arbeiten von Studenten, Hochschullehrern und anderen Akademikern als eBook und gedrucktes Buch. Die Verlagswebsite www.grin.com ist die ideale Plattform zur Veröffentlichung von Hausarbeiten, Abschlussarbeiten, wissenschaftlichen Aufsätzen, Dissertationen und Fachbüchern.

Visit us on the internet:

http://www.grin.com/

http://www.facebook.com/grincom

http://www.twitter.com/grin_com

TOWARDS A GREATER DEPRESSION?

Luis Enrique Ponce Goyochea

Abstract

Within the context of any financial crisis, government manipulation of the monetary base causes the downturn to last even longer than in the framework of a purely free market, thus leading to a sharper depression. From an *Austrian* viewpoint (Murray N. Rothbard 2000 [1963], 2008 [1983], 2009, 2010 [1963]), the ultimate cause of *business cycles* is the underlying distortion of *interest rates* through the interaction of two core *inflating mechanisms*: *commercial bank credit expansion* fueled by *fractional reserve banking* and government manipulation of the monetary base through *central banking*. In this sense, it is precisely the latter which allows the former to increase its influence beyond the natural free market constraints upon inflation.

1

Introduction

Throughout this paper, empirical evidence is analyzed as to how government interference in the economy has historically deepened rather than alleviated financial turbulences.

In this sense, we first place the focus on how it was the monetary expansion led through the 1930s that actually prolonged the *Great Depression* for over a decade.

Then we move on to outline an interpretation as to how the same mistakes that prolonged the *Great Depression* might turn the current recession into an even *Greater Depression*.

An Austrian View of the 1930s

The quintessence of *Austrian Business Cycle Theory,* as originally conceived by Ludwig von Mises (2009 [1953] [1912]), points to the fact that what ultimately leads to the occurrence of business cycles is not central banking per se but *fractional reserve banking*, the market limits upon which are to a great extent removed, as Rothbard (2008 [1983]: 125-139) explains, by the monopoly on the issue of money granted by the government to one single bank, allowing the rest to *inflate in unison* by systematically pyramiding on top of their legally required reserves.

Under such fractional reserve banking system, it would only take the slightest loss of confidence by customers to unfold the lack of actual reserves held by banks in order to meet their liabilities, which in this case would be greater than their assets, thus making banks insolvent on an accounting basis.

Empirical evidence on the Great Depression shows that after growing by roughly 25% between March 1919 and March 1933, the monetary base in the U.S. had already doubled from that point forward by April 1940, within the context of a decade over which growth in real terms experienced a downward trend in 1937-1938, as a reflection of what actually constituted just another phase of the original downturn starting back in 1929, clearly showing that the initial recession had never actually been over in the first place.

The monetary base doubled during the artificial rebound occurred between 1933 and 1939 (only interrupted by the aforementioned decline between 1937 and 1938), and on a more general basis nearly tripled between 1929 and 1940, as a result of such expansionary monetary policies:

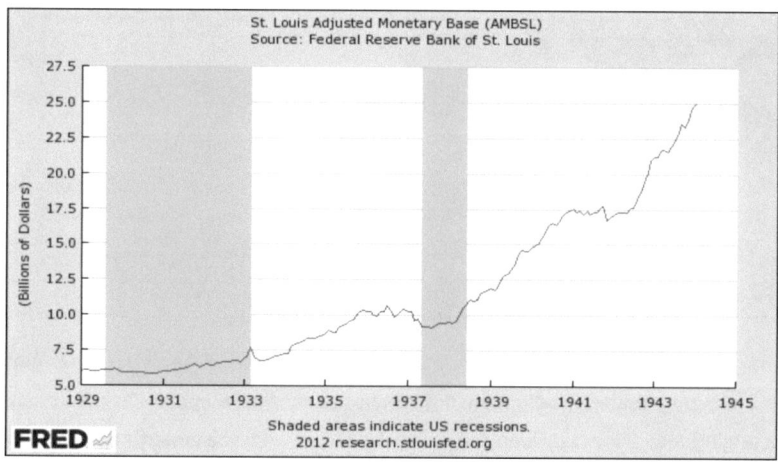

Hence, this clearly proves that the longer it takes for any recession to set in and properly foster the reallocation of resources otherwise wasted because of misleading signals after a preceding monetary expansion, the deeper should be the resulting depression.

This is exactly what happened throughout the 1930s, making the financial crash of 1929 into a much deeper and prolonged depression than it in fact might have been within the context of a truly free market.

Today´s Greater Depression

Over the past couple of decades, an unparalleled expansion of the monetary base has been set in motion, leading it to multiply by nearly 10 between 1990 and 2012:

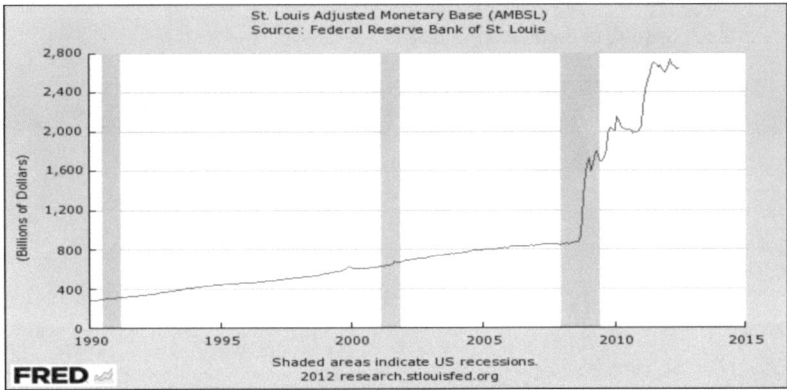

Looking further into the persistency of the ongoing crisis, it becomes clear that this lingering tendency ultimately derives from successive bubbles continuously emerging and bursting within the context of such unprecedented expansion of the monetary base in U.S. dollars, which has tripled from 2008 forward:

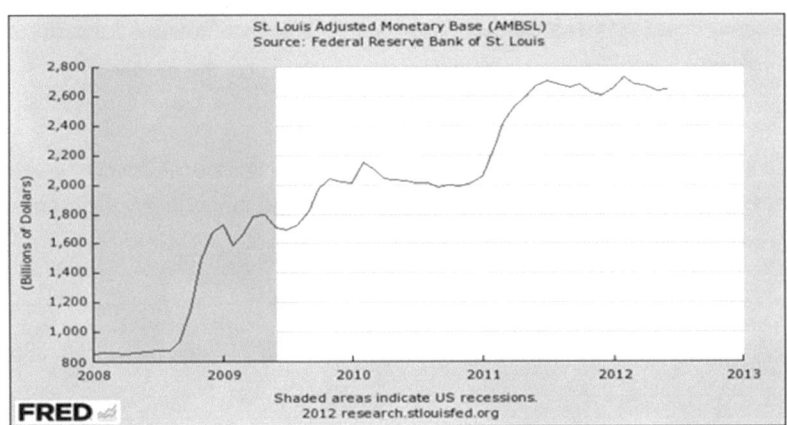

This bubble has been fostered by a series of systematic money injections into the economy, both indirectly through the manipulation of market interest rates and directly by subsequent rounds of *Quantitative Easing (QE)*.

As highlighted above, the monetary base tripled between 2008 and 2012, thus entailing a reminder of what the inflating process led to as from 1933 all the way through the setback of 1937-1938: it merely prolonged the recession already in progress since 1929, which ultimately evolved into what up until now has been known as the longest and deepest depression ever on record.

Comparing what happened back then to current events, the signal as to the effects that such tripling of the monetary base might exert towards the near future should not be overlooked, especially considering that the monetary expansion leading to the ongoing recession was performed on an even greater scale and thus its consequences might be even more damaging than they were after 1933, as might be the *Greater Depression* yet to unfold.

The Dollar Downward Trend

According to the Federal Reserve statistical release (H.4.1), official gold holdings amount to 11,041 million dollars, which is equivalent to merely 261,511,132.16 troy ounces in terms of physical gold, officially valued at $42.22 per troy ounce since 1974, all of which is officially reported to have been monetized.

Furthermore, considering that according to economic research data from the Federal Reserve Bank of St. Louis, by November 2012 the monetary base in U.S. dollars was 2,648.756 billions of dollars, then we may algebraically figure out that at such point in time every single troy ounce in existence in the vaults of the Fed was backing 10,128.65 dollars from the monetary base, nearly 6 times the market value of gold.

By such standard, the market value of gold should multiply nearly six-fold to accurately mirror the sharp decline undertaken by the purchasing power of the U.S. dollar in terms of the precious metal.

It is therefore pretty clear how government manipulation of the monetary base in terms of U.S. dollars has thus exerted a multiplying eroding effect on its exchange ratio against gold as compared to that reflected in the market value of the latter.

In this sense, the following graph depicts the amount of U.S. dollars backed per troy ounce of gold throughout the recent decade (2003-2012):

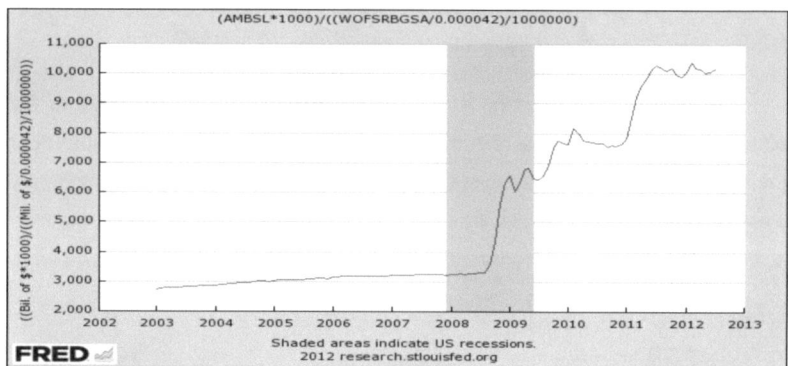

Over the last ten years, the market price of gold has risen four-fold on average (from below $400 in 2003 to over $1600 in 2012, peaking at market prices higher than $1,800 within the past couple of years), whereas the amount of U.S. dollars backed in terms of real assets per ounce of gold has multiplied nearly five-fold across the same period, to such an extent that a logical consequence arises as quite expectable given such facts: the relative proportion of the monetary base in U.S. dollars backed by gold has fallen sharply, from almost 40% to roughly 10%, i.e. the current gold-backing of the U.S. dollar has contracted to nearly a quarter of what it used to be ten years ago:

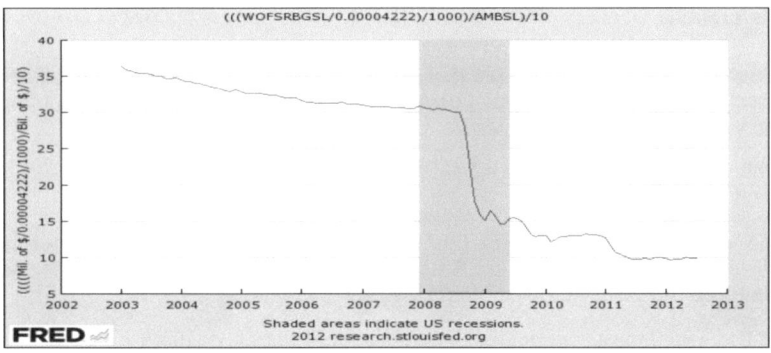

Conclusions

Allegedly *countercyclical policies* only lead to prolonging the *bubbles* derived from any inflating process, and eventually turn *recessions* into *depressions*.

This clearly shows that free market adjustment mechanisms constitute the only natural and sustainable way out of any distorting government interference resulting in *business cycles*.

In the light of the underlying monetary aspects of cyclical shocks, the *Mengerian* framework on money (Menger 2009 [1892]: 51-52) always reveals itself in real market dynamics concerning the natural evolution of exchange (Menger 2007 [1976] [1871]: 236-256), the means to which the most sustainable asset has proven to be gold.

References

Bastiat, Claude Frédéric (2011). *The Bastiat Collection (Pocket Paperback Edition)*. Auburn, Alabama: Ludwig von Mises Institute, available online at:

<http://library.mises.org/books/Frederic%20Bastiat/The%20Bastiat%20Collection.pdf>

Menger, Carl. (2007) [1976] [1871]. *Principles of Economics.* Arlington, Virginia: Institute for Human Studies, reprinted by the Ludwig von Mises Institute (Auburn, Alabama, 2007), available online at:

<http://library.mises.org/books/Carl%20Menger/Principles%20of%20Economics.pdf>

Menger, Carl. (2009) [1892]. *On the Origins of Money.* Auburn, Alabama: Ludwig von Mises Institute, available online at:
<http://library.mises.org/books/Carl%20Menger/On%20the%20Origins%20of%20Money.pdf>

Mises, Ludwig von. (1998). *Human Action: A Treatise on Economics (The Scholar´s Edition)*. Auburn, Alabama: Ludwig von Mises Institute, available online at:
<http://library.mises.org/books/Ludwig%20von%20Mises/Human%20Action.pdf>

Mises, Ludwig von. (2009) [1953] [1912]. *The Theory of Money and Credit.* New Haven: Yale University Press, available online at:

<http://library.mises.org/books/Ludwig%20von%20Mises/The%20Theory%20of%20Money%20and%20Credit.pdf>

Murphy, Robert P. (2011). *Study Guide to The Theory of Money and Credit (Ludwig von Mises).* Auburn, Alabama: Ludwig von Mises Institute, available online at:

<http://library.mises.org/books/Robert%20P%20Murphy/Study%20Guide%20to%20the%20Theory%20of%20Money%20and%20Credit.pdf>

Rothbard, Murray N. (2000) [1963]. *America´s Great Depression (Fifth Edition).* Auburn, Alabama: Ludwig von Mises Institute, available online at:

<http://library.mises.org/books/Murray%20N%20Rothbard/Americas%20Great%20Depression.pdf>

Rothbard, Murray N. (2008) [1983]. *The Mistery of Banking.* Auburn, Alabama: Ludwig von Mises Institute, available online at:

<http://library.mises.org/books/Murray%20N%20Rothbard/Mystery%20of%20Banking.pdf>

Rothbard, Murray N. (2009). *Economic Depressions: Their Cause and Cure.* Auburn, Alabama: Ludwig von Mises Institute, available online at:

<http://library.mises.org/books/Murray%20N%20Rothbard/Economic%20Depressions%20Their%20Cause%20and%20Cure.pdf>

Rothbard, Murray N. (2010) [1963]. *What Has Government Done to Our Money?* **Auburn, Alabama: Ludwig von Mises Institute, available online at:** <http://library.mises.org/books/Murray%20N%20Rothbard/What%20Has%20Government%20Done%20to%20Our%20Money.pdf>

Web Sources:

Official Website U.S. Bureau of Labor Statistics: CPI Inflation Calculator: <http://www.bls.gov/data/inflation_calculator.htm>

Official Website Federal Reserve Bank of St. Louis: Federal Reserve Economic Data (FRED): <http://research.stlouisfed.org/fred2/>

Official Website of the Board of Governors of the Federal Reserve System:

<http://www.federalreserve.gov>

<http://www.federalreserve.gov/releases/h41/Current/>

<http://www.federalreserve.gov/monetarypolicy/reservebalances_p.htm>

Official Website of BBC News: Market Data:

<http://www.bbc.co.uk/news/business/market_data/commodities/default.stm>

<http://www.bbc.co.uk/news/business/market_data/currency/default.stm>